Theories of Human Growth and Developmental Psychology

Contents

Page

2. Introduction to Developmental Psychology

4: Freud's Stages of Psychosexual Development

6: Erik Erikson's Theory of Psychosocial Development

8: Learning Theories (Behaviourist)

8: Social Child Development Theories

12: Cognitive Theories of Development

13: Piaget's Theory and Stages of Cognitive Development

14: Kohlberg's Theory of Moral Development

17: Erik Erikson's Stages of Development

19: Physical Developmental Milestones

21: Cognitive Developmental Milestones

24: Social Emotional Developmental Milestones

26: Early Childhood

27: Adolescence

28: Early Adulthood: Emerging Adulthood: Middle Adulthood

29: Old Age

29: Parenting Variables and Parenting Styles

30: Parenting Roles: Mother and Father Factors

31: Bowlby's Attachment Theory

32: Nature V's Nurture

37: References

Theories of Human Growth and Development
Developmental Psychology

Developmental psychology is the branch of psychology and the scientific study of how people grow and change over the course of a lifetime. Originally concerned with infants and children it expanded to include adolescence, adult development, ageing, and the entire lifespan. Beginning with Sigmund Freud (1856–1939) and Jean Piaget (1896–1980), the early focus of developmental psychology was on the maturation of children. Within the last three decades, researchers who study human development have expanded their focus to examine change across a broad range of topics including psycho-physiological processes; cognitive development involving areas such as problem solving, moral and conceptual understanding; language acquisition; social, personality, emotional development, self-concept and identity formation.

The scientific study of human growth and development is important not only to psychology, but also to biology, sociology, anthropology, education, history and health care. Most important, however, are its practical applications. By better understanding how and why people change and grow, the knowledge can be applied to help people to reach their full potential.

There have been a number of important debates and issues throughout the history of developmental psychology. Some of the major questions posed by psychologists and researchers are centred on the relative contributions of genetics versus environment and the **'Nature V's Nurture' debate**. Does genetic inheritance play a larger role in influencing development and behaviour, or does the environment have a stronger effect? Today, most psychologists recognize that both elements play an essential role, but the debate continues.

A second important consideration in developmental psychology involves the relative importance of early experiences versus those that occur later in life. Are we more affected by events that occur in early childhood, or do later events play an equally important role?

A third and major issue is that of continuity. Does change occur smoothly over time, or through a series of predetermined steps? Most theories of development fall under three broad areas: Psychoanalytical theories: Learning theories: Cognitive theories.

Psychoanalytic theories are those influenced by the work of Sigmund Freud (1856–1939), who believed in the importance of the unconscious mind and childhood experiences. Freud's contribution to developmental theory was his proposal that development occurs through a series of psychosexual stages

Theorist Erik Erikson (1902-1994) expanded upon Freud's ideas by proposing an 8 stage theory of psychosocial development. Erikson's theory focused on conflicts that arise at different stages of development and, unlike Freud's theory, Erikson described development throughout the lifespan.

Learning theories focus on how the environment impacts behaviour. Important learning processes include classical conditioning, operant conditioning and social learning. In each case, behaviour is shaped by the interaction between the individual and the environment.

Cognitive theories focus on the development of mental processes, skills, and abilities. Examples of cognitive theories include Jean Piaget's (1896-1980) theory of cognitive development.

Freud's Stages of Psychosexual Development

Proposed by psychoanalyst Sigmund Freud (1856–1939), the theory of psychosexual development describes how personality develops during childhood. While the theory is well-known in psychology, it is also one of the most controversial. Freud believed that personality develops through a series of childhood stages in which the pleasure-seeking energies of the id become focused on certain erogenous areas. This psychosexual energy or libido (sexual drives or instincts) is described as the driving force behind behaviour.

These are called psychosexual stages because each stage represents the fixation of libido on a different area of the body. As a person grows physically certain areas of their body become important as sources of potential frustration (erogenous zones), pleasure or both.

Freud believed that life was built round tension and pleasure. He also believed that all tension was due to the build up of libido (sexual energy) and that all pleasure came from its discharge.

In describing human personality development as psychosexual Freud meant to convey that what develops is the way in which sexual energy accumulates and is discharged as we mature biologically. Freud used the term 'sexual' in a very general way to mean all pleasurable actions and thoughts.

Freud stressed that the first five years of life are crucial to the formation of adult personality. The id must be controlled in order to satisfy social demands; this sets up a conflict between frustrated wishes and social norms.

The ego and superego develop in order to exercise this control and direct the need for gratification into socially acceptable channels. Gratification centres of different areas of the body at different stages of growth, making the conflict at each stage psychosexual.

Psychoanalytic theory suggested that personality is mostly established by the age of five. Early experiences play a large role in personality development and continue to influence behaviour later in life. If these psychosexual stages are completed successfully, the result is a healthy personality. If certain issues are not resolved at the appropriate stage, fixation can occur. A fixation is a persistent focus on an earlier psychosexual stage. Until this conflict is resolved, the individual will remain "stuck" in this stage. For example, a person who is fixated at the oral stage may be over-dependent on others and may seek oral stimulation through smoking, drinking, or eating.

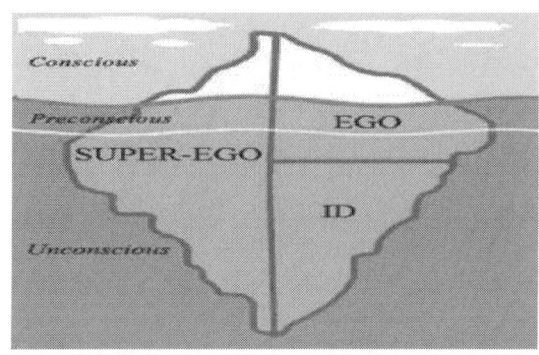 

Freud's Psychosexual Stages

Stage	Focus
Oral (0-18 months)	Pleasure centers on the mouth -- sucking, biting, chewing
Anal (18-36 months)	Pleasure focuses on bowel and bladder elimination; coping with demands for control
Phallic (3-6 years)	Pleasure zone is the genitals; coping with incestuous sexual feelings
Latency (6 to puberty)	Dormant sexual feelings
Genital (puberty on)	Maturation of sexual interests

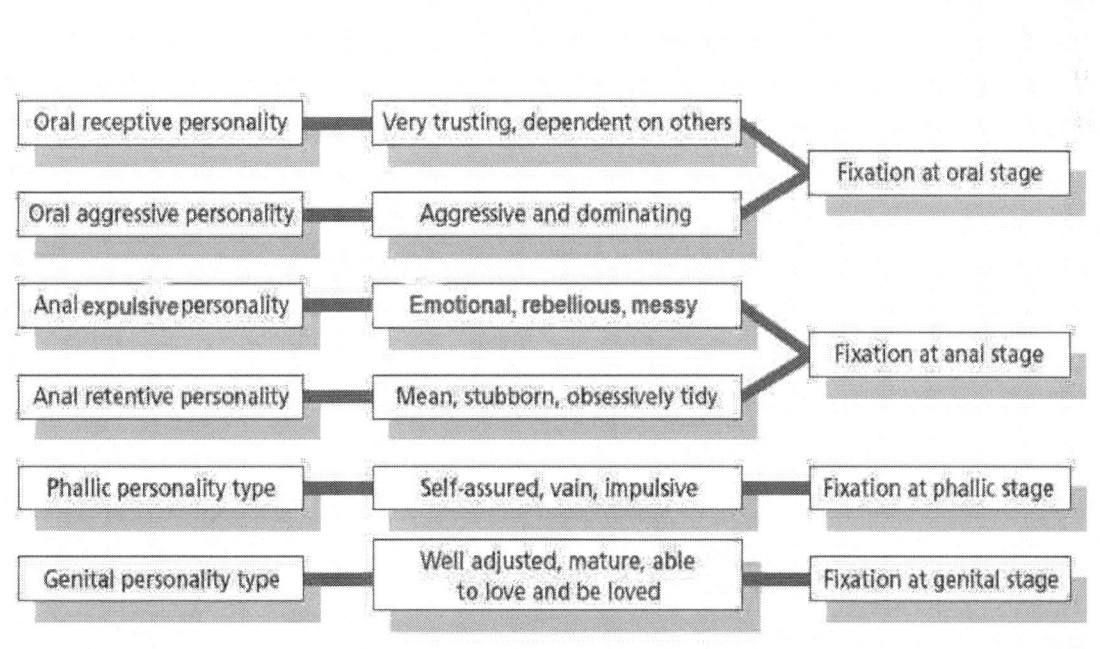

Erik Erikson's Theory of Psychosocial Development

Erik Erikson's (1902-1994) theory of psychosocial development is one of the best-known theories of personality in psychology. Much like Sigmund Freud, Erikson believed that personality develops in a series of stages. Unlike Freud's theory of psychosexual stages, Erikson's theory describes the impact of social experience across the whole lifespan.

One of the main elements of Erikson's psychosocial stage theory is the development of ego identity. Ego identity is the conscious sense of self that we develop through social interaction. According to Erikson, our ego identity is constantly changing due to new experiences and information we acquire in our daily interactions with others.

When psychologists talk about identity, they are referring to all of the beliefs, ideals, and values that help shape and guide a person's behaviour. The formation of identity is something that begins in childhood and becomes particularly important during adolescence, but it is a process that continues throughout life. Our personal identity gives each of us an integrated and cohesive sense of self that endures and continues to grow as we age.

In addition to ego identity, Erikson also believed that a sense of competence motivates behaviours and actions. Each stage in Erikson's theory is concerned with becoming competent in an area of life. If the stage is handled well, the person will feel a sense of mastery, which is sometimes referred to as ego strength or ego quality. If the stage is managed poorly, the person will emerge with a sense of inadequacy.

In each stage, Erikson believed people experience a conflict that serves as a turning point in development. In Erikson's view these conflicts are centred on either developing a psychological quality or failing to develop that quality. During these times, the potential for personal growth is high, but so is the potential for failure.

Erikson's Stage Theory in its Final Version

Age	Conflict	Resolution or "Virtue"	Culmination in old age
Infancy (0-1 year)	Basic trust vs. mistrust	Hope	Appreciation of interdependence and relatedness
Early childhood (1-3 years)	Autonomy vs. shame	Will	Acceptance of the cycle of life, from integration to disintegration
Play age (3-6 years)	Initiative vs. guilt	Purpose	Humor; empathy; resilience
School age (6-12 years)	Industry vs. Inferiority	Competence	Humility; acceptance of the course of one's life and unfulfilled hopes
Adolescence (12-19 years)	Identity vs. Confusion	Fidelity	Sense of complexity of life; merging of sensory, logical and aesthetic perception
Early adulthood (20-25 years)	Intimacy vs. Isolation	Love	Sense of the complexity of relationships; value of tenderness and loving freely
Adulthood (26-64 years)	Generativity vs. stagnation	Care	Caritas, caring for others, and agape, empathy and concern
Old age (65-death)	Integrity vs. Despair	Wisdom	Existential identity; a sense of integrity strong enough to withstand physical disintegration

Learning Theories

During the first half of the twentieth century, a new school of thought known as behaviourism rose to become a dominant force within psychology. Behaviourists believed that psychology needed to focus only on observable and quantifiable behaviours in order to become a more scientific discipline.

According to the behavioural perspective, all human behaviour can be described in terms of environmental influences. Some behaviourists, such as John B. Watson and B.F. Skinner, insisted that learning occurs purely through processes of association and reinforcement. Later, psychologist Albert Bandura rejected this narrow perspective and demonstrated the powerful effects of observational learning.

Classical Conditioning- is a process of behaviour modification by which a subject comes to respond in a desired manner to a previously neutral stimulus that has been repeatedly presented along with an unconditioned stimulus that elicits the desired response. **(Stimulus ->Response)**

Operant conditioning- is a method of learning that occurs through rewards and punishments for behaviour. Through these rewards and punishments, an association is made between behaviour and a consequence for that behaviour.

Social Child Development Theories

There is a great deal of research on the social development of children. John Bowbly proposed one of the earliest theories of social development. He believed that early relationships with caregivers play a major role in child development and continue to influence social relationships throughout life.

Social Learning Theory

The social learning theory proposed by **Albert Bandura** has become perhaps the most influential theory of learning and development. While rooted in many of the basic concepts of traditional learning theory, Bandura believed that direct reinforcement could not account for all types of learning.

His theory added a social element, arguing that people can learn new information and behaviours by watching other people. Known as observational learning (or modelling), this type of learning can be used to explain a wide variety of behaviours.

Basic Social Learning Concepts

There are three core concepts at the heart of social learning theory. First is the idea that people can learn through observation. Second is the idea that internal mental states are an essential part of this process. Thirdly, this theory recognizes that just because something has been learned, it does not mean that it will result in a change in behaviour.

Observational Learning

In his famous Bobo doll experiment, Bandura demonstrated that children learn and imitate behaviours they have observed in other people. Bandura *et al* (1963) carried out a classic study on observational learning or modelling- where young children were shown one of two films. One film showed a female adult behaving in an aggressive way towards a Bobo doll. The other film showed a female adult behaving non-aggressively. The children who had watched the adult behave aggressively were much more likely to attack the Bobo doll than those who had watched the non-aggressive film.

Bandura (1965) carried out another study on aggressive behaviour. One group of children were shown a film of an adult kicking and punching a Bobo doll. The 2nd group saw the same aggressive behaviour performed by the adult but this time the adult was rewarded by another adult for their behaviour. A 3rd group saw the same aggressive behaviour, but this time the adult was punished by another adult, who warned them not to be so aggressive in the future. Those children who had seen the model rewarded or seen the model neither rewarded nor punished- behaved much more aggressively to the doll than those who had seen the model punished.

Bandura identified three basic models of observational learning: A **live model**, which involves an actual individual demonstrating or acting out a behaviour: A **verbal instructional model** which involves descriptions and explanations of behaviour: A **symbolic model**, which involves real or fictional characters displaying behaviours in books, films, television programs, or online media.

Intrinsic Reinforcement

Bandura noted that external, environmental reinforcement was not the only factor to influence learning and behaviour. He described intrinsic reinforcement as a form of internal reward, such as pride, satisfaction, and a sense of accomplishment. This emphasis on internal thoughts and cognitions helps connect learning theories to cognitive developmental theories. While many textbooks place social learning theory with behavioural theories, Bandura himself describes his approach as a 'social cognitive theory.'

Learning does not necessarily lead to a change in behaviour. While behaviourists believe that learning leads to a permanent change in behaviour, observational learning demonstrates that people can learn new information without demonstrating new behaviours.

The Modelling Process

Not all observed behaviours are effectively learned. Factors involving both the model and the learner can play a role in whether social learning is successful. Certain requirements and steps must also be followed.

Attention:
In order to learn, you need to be paying attention. Anything that detracts your attention is going to have a negative effect on observational learning. If the model is interesting or there is a novel aspect to the situation, you are far more likely to dedicate your full attention to learning.

Retention:
The ability to store information is also an important part of the learning process. Retention can be affected by a number of factors, but the ability to pull up information later and act on it is vital to observational learning.

Reproduction:
Once you have paid attention to the model and retained the information, it is time to actually perform the behaviour you observed. Further practice of the learned behaviour leads to improvement and skill advancement.

Motivation:

Finally in order for observational learning to be successful, one has to be motivated to imitate the behaviour that has been modelled. Reinforcement and punishment play an important role in motivation. Experiencing these motivators can be highly effective, but so can observing others experience some type of reinforcement or punishment.

In addition to influencing other psychologists, Bandura's social learning theory has had important implication in the field of education. Today, both teachers and parents recognize the importance of modelling appropriate behaviours. Other classroom strategies such as encouraging children and building self-efficacy are also rooted in social learning theory.

Lev Vygotsky (1896-1934) proposed a seminal learning theory that has gone on to become very influential, especially in the field of education. Like Piaget, Vygotsky believed that children learn actively and through hands-on experiences. His socio-cultural theory also suggested that parents, caregivers, peers and the culture at large were responsible for the development of higher order functions.

Cognitive Theories

Cognitive theories of development examine how thought processes and mental operations influence growth and change. Although there is no general theory of cognitive development, the most historically influential theory was developed by Jean Piaget, a Swiss Psychologist (1896-1980).

His theory provided many central concepts in the field of developmental psychology and concerned the growth of intelligence, which for Piaget, meant the ability to more accurately represent the world, and perform logical operations on representations of concepts grounded in the world.

The theory concerns the emergence and acquisition of schemata - schemes of how one perceives the world - in "developmental stages", times when children are acquiring new ways of mentally representing information.

The theory is considered "constructivist", meaning that, unlike nativist theories (which describe cognitive development as the unfolding of innate knowledge and abilities) or empiricist theories (which describe cognitive development as the gradual acquisition of knowledge through experience), it asserts that we construct our cognitive abilities through self-motivated action in the world.

Jean Piaget created one of the most famous theories of cognitive development, suggesting that children are not just passive recipients of information. Instead, he proposed that children are little scientists" who actively construct their knowledge and understanding of the world. Piaget's theory of cognitive development accounts for the steps and sequence of children's intellectual development.

Table 2.1
Piaget's Four Stages of Cognitive Development

Stage	Description	Age Range
Sensorimotor	An infant progresses from reflexive, instinctual action at birth to the beginning of symbolic thought. The infant constructs an understanding of the world by coordinating sensory experiences with physical actions.	Birth to 2 years
Preoperational	The child begins to represent the world with words and images; these words and images reflect increased symbolic thinking and go beyond the connection of sensory information and physical action.	2 to 7 years
Concrete operational	The child can now reason logically about concrete events and classify objects into different sets.	7 to 11 years
Formal operational	The adolescent reasons in more abstract and logical ways. Thought is more idealistic.	11 to 15 years

Piaget's Theory

Stage	Age Range	Description
Sensorimotor	0-2 years	Coordination of senses with motor response, sensory curiosity about the world. Language used for demands and cataloguing. Object permanence developed
Preoperational	2-7 years	Symbolic thinking, use of proper syntax and grammar to express full concepts. Imagination and intuition are strong, but complex abstract thought still difficult. Conservation developed.
Concrete Operational	7-11 years	Concepts attached to concrete situations. Time, space, and quantity are understood and can be applied, but not as independent concepts
Formal Operations	11+	Theoretical, hypothetical, and counterfactual thinking. Abstract logic and reasoning. Strategy and planning become possible. Concepts learned in one context can be applied to another.

Kohlberg's Theory of Moral Development

Moral development is a major topic of interest in both psychology and education. One of the best known theories was developed by psychologist Lawrence Kohlberg (1927-1987) who modified and expanded upon Jean Piaget's work to form a theory that explained the **development of moral reasoning**.

Piaget described a two-stage process of moral development, while Kohlberg's theory of moral development outlined **six stages within three different levels.** Kohlberg extended Piaget's theory, proposing that moral development is a continual process that occurs throughout the lifespan.

Kohlberg based his theory upon research and interviews with groups of young children. A series of moral dilemmas were presented to these participants and they were also interviewed to determine the reasoning behind their judgments of each scenario.

"The Heinz Dilemma"

A woman was near death from cancer. There was one drug that the doctors thought might save her. It was a form of radium that a chemist in the same town had recently discovered. The drug was expensive to make, but the chemist was charging ten times what the drug cost him to make.

He paid $200 for the radium and charged $2,000 for a small dose of the drug. The sick woman's husband, Heinz, went to everyone he knew to borrow the money, but he could only get together about $ 1,000 which is half of what it cost. He told the chemist that his wife was dying and asked him to sell it cheaper or let him pay later. But the chemist said: "No, I discovered the drug and I'm going to make money from it." So Heinz got desperate and broke into the man's store to steal the drug-for his wife. Should the husband have done that?" (Kohlberg, 1963).

Kohlberg was not interested so much in the answer to the question of whether Heinz was wrong or right, but in the *reasoning* for each participant's decision. The responses were then classified into various stages of reasoning in his theory of moral development.

Level 1: Pre-conventional Morality

Stage one: Obedience and Punishment:

The earliest stage of moral development is especially common in young children, but adults are also capable of expressing this type of reasoning. At this stage, children see rules as fixed and absolute. Obeying the rules is important because it is a means to avoid punishment.

Stage 2 - Individualism and Exchange

At this stage of moral development, children account for individual points of view and judge actions based on how they serve individual needs. In the Heinz dilemma, children argued that the best course of action was the choice that best-served Heinz's needs. Reciprocity is possible at this point in moral development, but only if it serves one's own interests.

Level 2: Conventional Morality

Stage 3: Interpersonal Relationships

Often referred to as the "good boy-good girl" orientation, this stage of moral development is focused on living up to social expectations and roles. There is an emphasis on conformity, being "nice," and consideration of how choices influence relationships.

Stage 4: Maintaining Social Order

At this stage of moral development, people begin to consider society as a whole when making judgments. The focus is on maintaining law and order by following the rules, doing one's duty and respecting authority.

Level 3: Post-conventional Morality

Stage 5: Social Contract and Individual Rights

At this stage, people begin to account for the differing values, opinions and beliefs of other people. Rules of law are important for maintaining a society, but members of the society should agree upon these standards.

Stage 6: Universal Principles

Kolhberg's final level of moral reasoning is based upon universal ethical principles and abstract reasoning. At this stage, people follow these internalized principles of justice, even if they conflict with laws and rules.

Criticisms of Kohlberg's Theory of Moral Development:

Does moral reasoning necessarily lead to moral behaviour? Kohlberg's theory is concerned with moral thinking, but there is a big difference between knowing what we *ought* to do versus our actual actions.

Is justice the only aspect of moral reasoning we should consider? Critics have pointed out that Kohlberg's theory of moral development overemphasizes the concept as justice when making moral choices. Factors such as compassion, caring and other interpersonal feelings may play an important part in moral reasoning.

Does Kohlberg's theory overemphasize Western philosophy? Individualistic cultures emphasize personal rights while collectivist cultures stress the importance of society and community. Eastern cultures may have different moral outlooks that Kohlberg's theory does not account for.

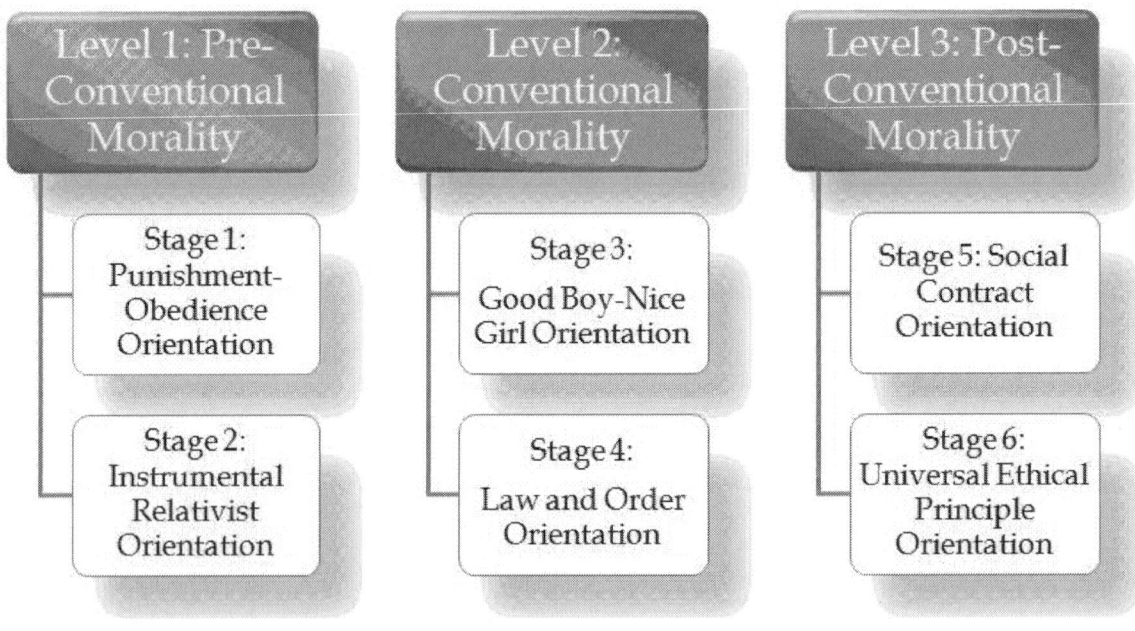

Erickson's Stages of Development

Erik Erickson (1902-1994) a German born American developmental psychologist and psychoanalyst is famous for his theories on psycho-social and physical development.

Erickson's Stages of Development- Lifespan

Stage:	Conflict	Events	Outcome
Infancy to 18 months	Trust vs. Mistrust	Feeding	Develop trust when caregivers respond; mistrust when they don't.
Early Childhood 2–3 years	Autonomy vs. Shame & Doubt	Toilet Training	Develop a sense of personal control. Success-autonomy Failure-shame, doubt
Pre-school 3–5 years	Initiative vs. Guilt	Exploration	Asserting power and control over environment. Success-sense of purpose. Failure-disapproval, guilt.
School age 6–11 years	Industry vs. Inferiority	School	Cope with new academic and social demands. Success-competence. Failure-weak self-image.
Adolescence 12–18 years	Identity vs. Role Confusion	Social Relationships	Develop "self." Success-true to yourself. Failure-confusion and weak self.
Young Adult 19–40 years	Intimacy vs. Isolation	Relationships	Loving relationships. Success-strong relationships. Failure-loneliness.
Middle Age 41–64	Generativity vs. Stagnation	Work & Parenthood	Need to create and nurture. Success-usefulness and accomplishment. Failure-withdrawal.
Maturity 65–death	Ego Integrity vs. Despair	Reflection on Life	Success-feelings of wisdom Failure- regret, bitterness and despair

(Erikson, 1968)

Erickson's Stages of Psychosocial Development

Erikson's Stages of Psychosocial Development

Stage	Ages				What issues concern the child at this stage?
Stage One	Infancy-1 year	Trust	versus	Mistrust	If needs are met, child develops a sense of trust
Stage Two	1-2year	Autonomy	versus	Shame	Develops a need to do things for themselves or will doubt their abilities
Stage Three	3-5years	Initiative	versus	Guilt	Initiate and carry out tasks or feel guilty for not being independent (potty training?)
Stage Four	6-adolescence	Industry (Competence)	versus	Inferiority	Gain pleasure form applying themselves or feel inferior (Do I have worth?)
Stage Five	Adolescence	Identiy	versus	Identity Confusion	Testing roles and integrating to form a single identity or will be confused about self
Stage Six	Young adult	Intimacy	versus	Isolation	Forming close, intimate relationships or feel socially isolated
Stage Seven	Middle adult	Generativity	versus	Stagnation	Develop of sense of contribution to the world or feel lack of purpose
Stage Eight	Late adult	Ego Integrity	versus	Ego Despair	Have I lived a full life? Satisfaction or failure?

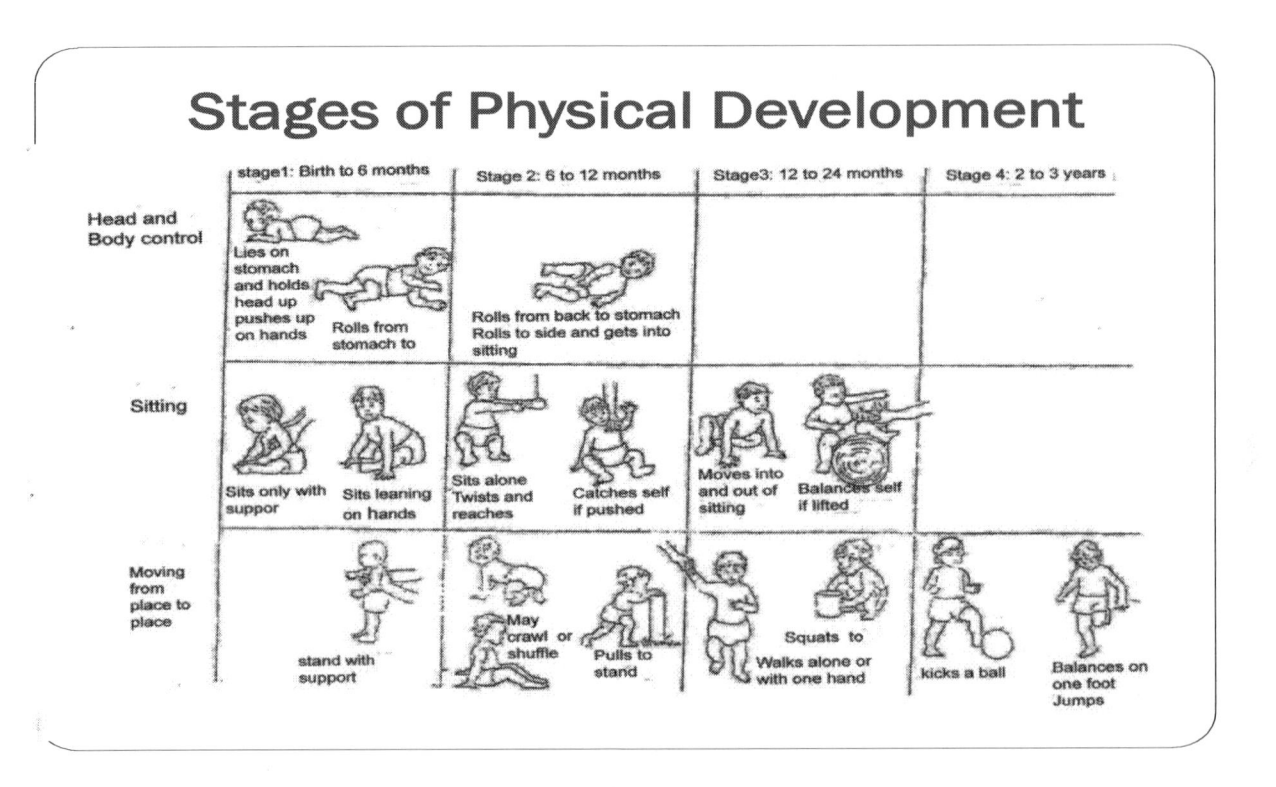

Stages of Physical Development

	stage1: Birth to 6 months	Stage 2: 6 to 12 months	Stage3: 12 to 24 months	Stage 4: 2 to 3 years
Head and Body control	Lies on stomach and holds head up pushes up on hands; Rolls from stomach to	Rolls from back to stomach; Rolls to side and gets into sitting		
Sitting	Sits only with support; Sits leaning on hands	Sits alone Twists and reaches; Catches self if pushed	Moves into and out of sitting; Balances self if lifted	
Moving from place to place		stand with support; May crawl or shuffle	Pulls to stand; Squats to Walks alone or with one hand	kicks a ball; Balances on one foot Jumps

18

Physical Developmental Milestones

Physical developmental milestones are abilities that most children are able to perform by a certain age. During the first year of a child's life, physical milestones are centred on the infant learning to master self-movement, hold objects and hand-to-mouth coordination.

From Birth to 3 Months

- At this age, most babies begin to:
- Use rooting, sucking and grasping reflexes
- Slightly raise the head when lying on the stomach
- Hold head up for a few seconds with support
- Clench hands into fists
- Tug and pull on their own hands
- Repeat body movements

From 3 to 6 Months

At this age, babies begin to develop greater agility and strength. They:

- Roll over
- Pull their bodies forward
- Pull themselves up by grasping the edge of the crib
- Reach for and grasp object
- Bring object they are holding to their mouths
- Shake and play with objects

From 6 to 9 Months

During this time, children become increasingly mobile. They usually begin to:

- Crawl
- Grasp and pull object toward their own body
- Transfer toys and objects from one hand to the other

From 9 to 12 Months

In addition to the major milestones such as standing up and walking, children also begin to develop more advanced fine-motor skills. In this window of development, most babies are able to:

- Sit up unaided
- Stand without assistance
- Walk without help

- Pick up and throw objects
- Roll a ball
- Pick up objects between their thumb and one finger

From 1 to 2 Years

Children become increasingly independent and this age and tasks requiring balance and hand-eye coordination begin to emerge. During this stage of development, most children are able to:

- Pick things up while standing up
- Walk backwards
- Walk up and down stair without assistance
- Move and sway to music
- Colour or paint by moving the entire arm
- Scribble with markers or crayons
- Turn knobs and handles

From 2 to 3 Years

Building on earlier skills, children become increasingly adept at activities that require coordination and speed. From one to three years of age, most children:

- Run in a forward direction
- Jump in one place
- Kick a ball
- Stand on one foot
- Turn pages of a book
- Draw a circle
- Hold a crayon between the thumb and fingers

From 3 to 4 Years

Physical abilities become more advanced as children develop better movement and balance skills. From age three to four, most children begin to:

- Ride a tricycle
- Go down a slide without help
- Throw and catch a ball
- Pull and steer toys
- Walk in a straight line
- Build a tall towers with toy blocks
- Manipulate clay into shapes

From 4 to 5 Years

During this period of development, children become increasingly confident in their abilities. Most children begin to:

- Jump on one foot
- Walk backwards
- Do somersaults
- Cut paper with safety scissors
- Print some letters
- Copy shapes including squares and crosses

Cognitive Developmental Milestones

From Birth to 3 Months

Major developmental milestones at this age are centred on exploring the basic senses and learning more about the body and the environment. During this period, most infants begin to:

- See objects more clearly within a distance of 13 inches
- Focus on moving objects, including the faces of caregivers
- Tell between sweet, salty, bitter and sour tastes
- Detect differences in pitch and volume
- See all colours in the human visual spectrum
- Respond to their environment with facial expressions
- Demonstrate anticipatory behaviours like rooting and sucking at the site of a nipple or bottle

From 3 to 6 Months

In early infancy, perceptual abilities are still developing. From the age of three to six months, infants begin to develop a stronger sense of perception. At this age, most babies begin to:

- Recognize familiar faces
- Respond to the facial expressions of other people
- Recognize and react to familiar sounds
- Begin to imitate facial expressions

From 6 to 9 Months

To learn more about the mental processes of infants, researchers have come up with a number of creative tasks that reveal the inner workings of the baby brain. From the age of six to nine months, researchers have found that most infants begin to:

- Understand the differences between animate and inanimate objects
- Tell the differences between pictures depicting different numbers of objects
- Utilize the relative size of an object to determine how far away it is
- Gaze longer at "impossible" things, such as an object suspended in midair

From 9 to 12 Months

As infants become more physically adept, they are able to explore the world around them in greater depth. Sitting up, crawling, and walking are just a few of the physical milestones that allow babies to gain a greater mental understanding of the world around them. As they approach one year of age, most infants are able to:

- Understand the concept of object permanence, the idea that an object continues to exist even though it cannot be seen
- Imitate gestures and some basic actions
- Respond with gestures and sounds
- Like looking at picture books
- Manipulate objects by turning them over, trying to put one object into another

From 1 Year to 2 Years

After reaching a year of age, children's physical, social, and cognitive development seems to grow by leaps and bounds. Children at this age spend a tremendous amount of time observing the actions of adults, so it is important for parents and caregivers to set good examples for behaviour. Most one-year-olds begin to:

- Understand and respond to words
- Identify objects that are similar
- Tell the difference between "Me" and "You"
- Imitate the actions and language of adults
- Can point out familiar objects and people in a picture book
- Learn through exploration

From 2 to 3 Years

At two years of age, children are becoming increasingly independent. Since they are now able to better explore the world, a great deal of learning during this stage is the result of their own experiences.

- Sort objects by category (i.e., animals, flowers, trees, etc.)
- Stack rings on a peg from largest to smallest
- Imitate more complex adult actions (playing house, pretending to do laundry, etc.)
- Identify their own reflection in the mirror by name
- Respond to simple directions from parents and caregivers
- Name objects in a picture book
- Match objects with their uses

From 3 to 4 Years

Children become increasingly capable of analyzing the world around them in more complex ways. As they observe things, they begin to sort and categorize them into different categories, often referred to as schemas. Since children are becoming much more active in the learning process, they also begin to pose questions about the world around them. " At the age of three, most children are able to:

- Demonstrate awareness of the past and present
- Actively seek answers to questions
- Learn by observing and listening to instructions
- Organize objects by size and shape
- Understand how to group and match object according to colour
- Have a longer attention span of around 5 to 15 minutes
- Asks "why" questions to gain information

From 4 to 5 Years

As they near school age, children become better at using words, imitating adult actions, counting and other basic activities that are important for school preparedness. Most four-year-olds are able to:

- Rhyme
- Name and identify many colours
- Draw the shape of a person
- Count to five
- Tell where they live
- Draw pictures that they often name and describe

Social Emotional Milestones

While physical developmental milestones are often some of the easiest to observe, the early years of a child's life are also marked by other developmental milestones, including social and emotional ones. In many cases, these achievements can be difficult or even impossible to identify directly since they often involve such things as increased self-awareness. Such skills can be difficult to see, but they are just as important as the physical milestones, especially since social and emotional skills become so important once a child enters school.

From Birth to 3 Months

During the first three months, babies are actively learning about themselves and the people around them. Part of this skill-building involves:

- Looking at their own hands and sucking on fingers
- Looking at the part of their body that a parents or caregiver is touching
- Understanding how the legs and arms are attached
- Realizing that they are separate beings from those around them
- Learning to be comforted and soothed by adults
- Enjoying social stimulation and smiling at people
- Responding to touch

From 3 to 6 Months

Social interaction becomes increasingly important. During this period of development, most babies begin to:

- Respond when their name is called
- Smile
- Laugh
- Play peek-a-boo

From 6 to 9 Months

As babies get older, they may begin to show a preference for familiar people. Between the ages of six to nine months, most children can:

- Express a number of emotions including happiness, sadness, fear, and anger
- Distinguish between familiar family and friends and strangers
- Show frustration when a toy is taken away
- Respond to spoken words and gestures

From 9 to 12 Months

As children become more social, they often begin to mimic the actions of others. Self-regulation also becomes increasingly important at the child approaches one year of age. Most children can:

- Hold a cup and drink with help
- Imitate simple actions
- Feed themselves small bites of food
- Express anxiety when separated from parents or caregivers

From 1 to 2 Years

From the age of one to two years, kids often spend more time interacting with a wider range of people. They also start to gain a greater sense of self-awareness. At this stage, most can:

- Recognize their own image in the mirror
- Initiate play activities
- Play independently, often imitating adult actions
- Act pleased when the accomplish something
- Start trying to help, often by putting toys away
- Express negative emotions including anger and frustration
- Become more self-assertive and may try to direct the actions of others

From 2 to 3 Years

During the toddler years, children become more and more creative and confident. At two years old, most children begin to:

- Become aware that they are a boy or girl
- Begin to dress and undress themselves
- Demonstrate personal preferences about toys, food, and activities
- Start saying "No" to adults
- Enjoy watching and playing with other children
- Become defensive about their own possessions
- Use objects symbolically during play
- Often have rapid changes in mood

From 3 to 4 Years

Because three-year-olds are becoming increasingly able to perform physical actions, their sense of confidence and independence becomes more pronounced at this age. During the third year, most children begin to:

- Follow directions
- Perform some tasks with little or no assistance
- Share toys with other children
- Make up games and ask other children to join in
- Begin engaging in pretend play

From 4 to 5 Years

During the fourth year, children gain a greater awareness of their own individuality. As their physical skills increase, they are more capable of exploring their own abilities which can help lead to great confidence and personal pride. At this age, most children begin to:

- Understand basic differences between good and bad behaviour
- Develop friendships with other kids
- Compare themselves to other children and adults
- Become more aware of other people's feelings
- Enjoy dramatic, imaginative play with other children
- Enjoy competitive games

Early Childhood

Early childhood is often referred to as "pre-school age," "exploratory age" or "toy age." When children attend preschool, they broaden their social horizons and become more engaged with those around them. Impulses are channelled into fantasies, which leaves the task of the caretaker to balance eagerness for pursuing adventure, creativity and self-expression with the development of responsibility. If caretakers are properly encouraging and consistently disciplinary, children are more likely to develop positive self-esteem while becoming more responsible, and will follow through on assigned activities.

As children grow their past experiences will shape who they are, and allow them to perceive the world in their own way. If not allowed to decide which activities to perform, children may begin to feel guilt upon contemplating taking initiative. This negative association with independence will lead them to let others make decisions in place of them.

During a child's preschool and beginning school years, intelligence is demonstrated through logical and systematic manipulation of symbols related to concrete objects. Operational thinking develops which means actions are reversible, and egocentric thought diminishes. Children go through the transition from the world at home to that of school and peers. Children learn to make things, use tools, and acquire the skills to be a worker and a potential provider. Children can now receive feedback from outsiders about their accomplishments.

If children can discover pleasure in their activities, including their intellectual stimulation, most importantly in learning reading, writing, and basic maths, they will develop a sense of competence. If they are not successful or cannot discover pleasure in the process, they may develop a sense of inferiority and feelings of inadequacy that may haunt them throughout life. This is when children think of themselves as industrious or as inferior.

Adolescence

Adolescence is the period of life between the onset of puberty and the full commitment to an adult social role. It is the period known for the **formation of personal and social identity** (Erik Erikson) and the **discovery of moral purpose** (William Damon). Intelligence is demonstrated through the logical use of symbol is related to abstract concepts and formal reasoning.

A return to egocentric thought often occurs early in the period. Only 35% develop the capacity to reason formally during adolescence. (Huitt *et al* 1998)

Adolescence is divided into three parts: Early Adolescence: 9 to 13 years: Mid Adolescence: 13 to 15 years: Late Adolescence: 15 to 18 years. The adolescent unconsciously explores questions such as **"Who am I? Who do I want to be?"** Like toddlers, adolescents must explore, test limits, become autonomous, and commit to an identity, or sense of self. Different roles, behaviours and ideologies must be tried out to select an identity. Role confusion and inability to choose vocation can result from a failure to achieve a sense of identity.

Early Adulthood

Early adulthood, according to theorists such as Erik Erikson, is a stage where development is mainly focused on maintaining relationships. Examples include creating bond of intimacy, sustaining friendships, and ultimately making a family. Some theorists state that development of intimacy skills rely on the resolution of previous developmental stages. A sense of identity gained in the previous stages is also necessary for intimacy to develop. If this skill is not learned the alternative is alienation, isolation, a fear of commitment, and the inability to depend on others.

Emerging Adulthood

A related framework for this part of the life span is that of emerging adulthood. This concept suggests that people transition after their teenage years into a period not characterized as relationship building and an overall sense of constancy with life, but with years of living with parents, phases of self-discovery, and experimentation.

Middle Adulthood

Middle adulthood generally refers to the period between ages 25 to 69. During this period, middle-aged adults experience a conflict between generativity and stagnation. They may either feel a sense of contributing to society, the next generation or their immediate community or a sense of purposelessness. Physically, the middle-aged experience a decline in muscular strength, reaction time, sensory keenness, and cardiac output. Women experience the menopause and a sharp drop in the hormone oestrogen. Men experience an equivalent endocrine system event to menopause. Andropause in males is a hormone fluctuation with physical and psychological effects that can be similar to those seen in menopausal females. As men age, lowered testosterone levels can contribute to mood swings and a decline in sperm count and sexual function and responsiveness can be affected.

Old Age

This stage generally refers to those aged over 70. According to Erikson's Theory of Psychosocial Development, old age is the stage in which individuals assess the quality of their lives. In reflecting on their lives, people in this age group develop a feeling of integrity if deciding that their lives were successful or a feeling of despair if evaluation of one's life indicates a failure to achieve goals.

Physically, older people experience a decline in muscular strength, reaction time, stamina, hearing, distance perception, and the sense of smell. They also are more susceptible to illnesses such as cancer and pneumonia due to a weakened immune system. Programs aimed at balance, muscle strength, and mobility has been shown to reduce disability among mildly (but not more severely) disabled elderly.

Sexual expression depends in large part upon the emotional and physical health of the individual. Many older adults continue to be sexually active and satisfied with their sexual activity,

Mental disintegration may also occur, leading to dementia or ailments such as Alzheimer's disease. It is generally believed that **crystallized intelligence** (knowledge and skills that are accumulated over a lifetime) increases up to old age, while **fluid intelligence** (Fluid intelligence to the ability to reason quickly and to think abstractly) decreases with age. Whether or not normal intelligence increases or decreases with age depends on the measure and study. Longitudinal studies show that speed declines. Some cross-sectional studies suggest that intellect is stable.

Parenting Variables and Parenting Styles

Parenting variables alone have typically accounted for 20 to 50 percent of the variance in child outcomes.

Parenting styles

Authoritative Parenting is characterized as those parents who have high parental warmth, responsiveness, and demand, and who rate low in negativity and conflict. These parents are assertive but not intrusive or overly restrictive. This method of parenting is associated with more positive social and academic outcomes.

Authoritarian parenting is characterized by low levels of warmth and responsiveness with high levels of demanding and firm control. These parents focus on obedience and they monitor their children regularly. In general, this style of parenting is associated with maladaptive outcomes. The outcomes are more harmful for middle class boys than girls, preschool white girls than preschool black girls, and for white boys than Hispanic boys. Furthermore, the negative effects of authoritarian parenting among Asian Americans can be offset by positive peer support. Finally, among African Americans, some elements of authoritarian parenting such as firm control and physical discipline do not serve as predictive factors for negative outcomes.

Permissive parenting is characterized by high levels of responsiveness combined with low levels of demand. These parents are lenient and do not necessarily require mature behaviour. They allow for a high degree of self-regulation and typically avoid confrontation. Compared to children raised using the authoritative style, preschool girls raised in permissive families are less assertive. Additionally, preschool children of both sexes are less cognitively competent than those children raised under authoritative parenting styles

Rejecting or neglectful parenting is the final category. This is characterized by low levels of demanding and responsiveness. These parents are typically disengaged in their child's lives, lacking structure in their parenting styles and are unsupportive. Children in this category are typically the least competent of all the categories.

Parenting Roles: Mother and Father Factors

Parenting roles in child development have typically focused on the role of the mother. Recent literature, however, has looked toward the father as having an important role in child development. Affirming a role for fathers, studies have shown that children as young as 15 months benefit significantly from substantial engagement with their father. In particular, studies in the U.S. and New Zealand found the presence of the natural father was the most significant factor in reducing rates of early sexual activity and rates of teenage pregnancy in girls.

Another argument is that neither a mother nor a father is actually essential in successful parenting, and that single parents as well as homosexual couples can support positive child outcomes. According to this set of research, children need at least one consistently responsible adult with whom the child can have a positive emotional connection. Having more than one of these figures contributes to a higher likelihood of positive child outcomes.

Another parental factor often debated in terms of its effects on child development is divorce. Divorce in itself is not a determining factor of negative child outcomes. In fact, the majority of children from divorced families fall into the normal range on measures of psychological and cognitive functioning. A number of mediating factors play a role in determining the effects divorce has on a child; for example, divorcing families with young children often face harsher consequences in terms of demographic, social, and economic changes than do families with older children.

Positive co-parenting after divorce is part of a pattern associated with positive child coping, while hostile parenting behaviours lead to a destructive pattern leaving children at risk. Additionally, direct parental relationship with the child also affects the development of a child after a divorce. Overall, protective factors facilitating positive child development after a divorce are maternal warmth, positive father-child relationship, and cooperation between parents.

Attachment Theory

Attachment theory, originally developed by John Bowlby (1907-1990), focuses on the importance of open, intimate, emotionally meaningful relationships. Attachment is described as a biological system or powerful survival impulse that evolved to ensure the survival of the infant. A child who is threatened or stressed will move toward caregivers who create a sense of physical, emotional and psychological safety for the individual. Attachment feeds on body contact and familiarity. Later Mary Ainsworth developed the Strange Situation protocol and the concept of the secure base. There are four types of attachment styles: Secure: Anxious-avoidant: Anxious-resistant: Disorganized.

Secure attachment is a healthy attachment between the infant and the caregiver. It is characterized by trust.

Anxious-avoidant is an insecure attachment between an infant and a caregiver. This is characterized by the infant's indifference toward the caregiver.

Anxious-resistant is an insecure attachment between the infant and the caregiver characterized by distress from the infant when separated and anger when reunited.

Disorganized is an attachment style without a consistent pattern of responses upon return of the parent.

A child can be hindered in its natural tendency to form attachments. Some babies are raised without the stimulation and attention of a regular caregiver, or under conditions of abuse or extreme neglect. The possible short-term effects of this deprivation are anger, despair, detachment, and temporary delay in intellectual development. Long-term effects include increased aggression, clinging behaviour, detachment, psychosomatic disorders, and an increased risk of depression as an adult.

Nature V's Nurture

The **Nature V's Nurture** debate is one of the oldest issues in psychology. This debate is concerned with the extent to which particular aspects of behaviour are a product of either inherited (i.e. genetic) or acquired (i.e. learned) characteristics. Nature is that which is inherited or genetic. Nurture refers to all environmental influences after conception, i.e. experience.

Nature V Nurture

Nature/Nurture and Human Development

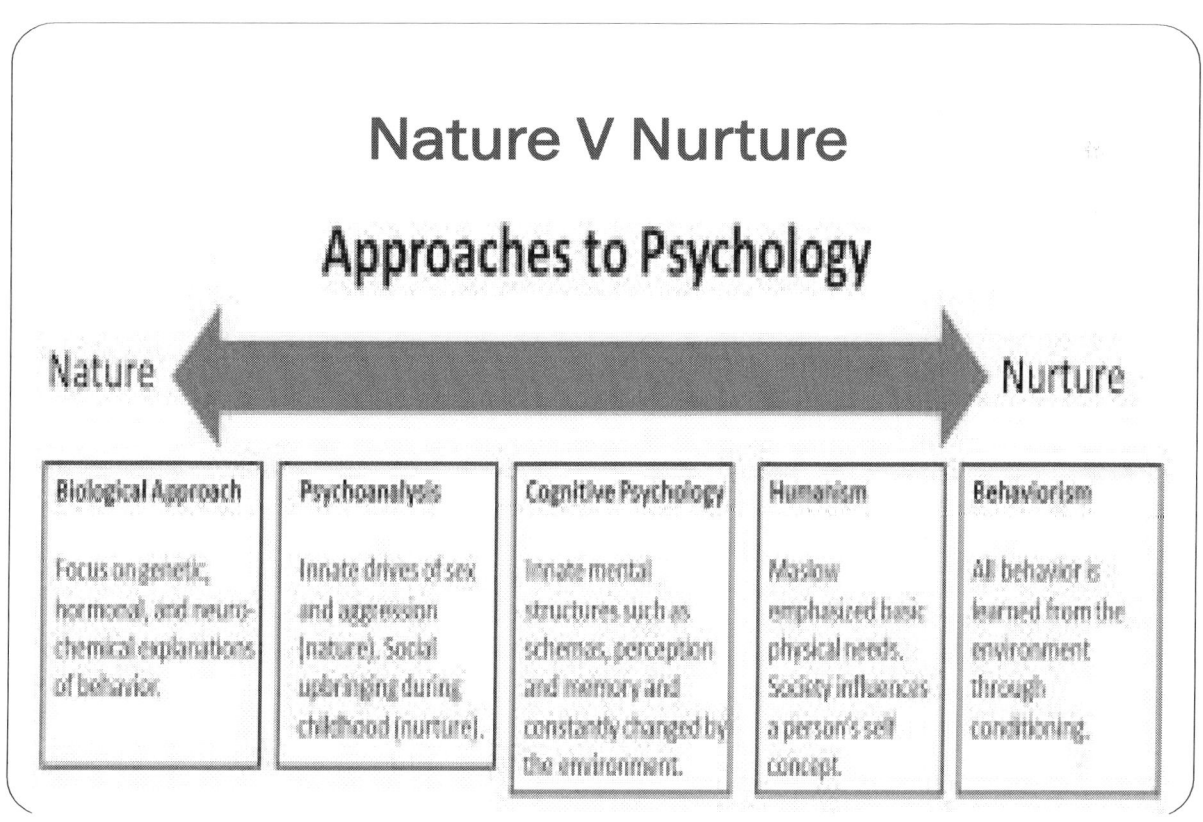

Nature V Nurture

Approaches to Psychology

Nature ←——————————————————→ Nurture

Biological Approach	Psychoanalysis	Cognitive Psychology	Humanism	Behaviorism
Focus on genetic, hormonal, and neuro-chemical explanations of behavior.	Innate drives of sex and aggression (nature). Social upbringing during childhood (nurture).	Innate mental structures such as schemas, perception and memory and constantly changed by the environment.	Maslow emphasized basic physical needs. Society influences a person's self concept.	All behavior is learned from the environment through conditioning.

Nature V Nurture

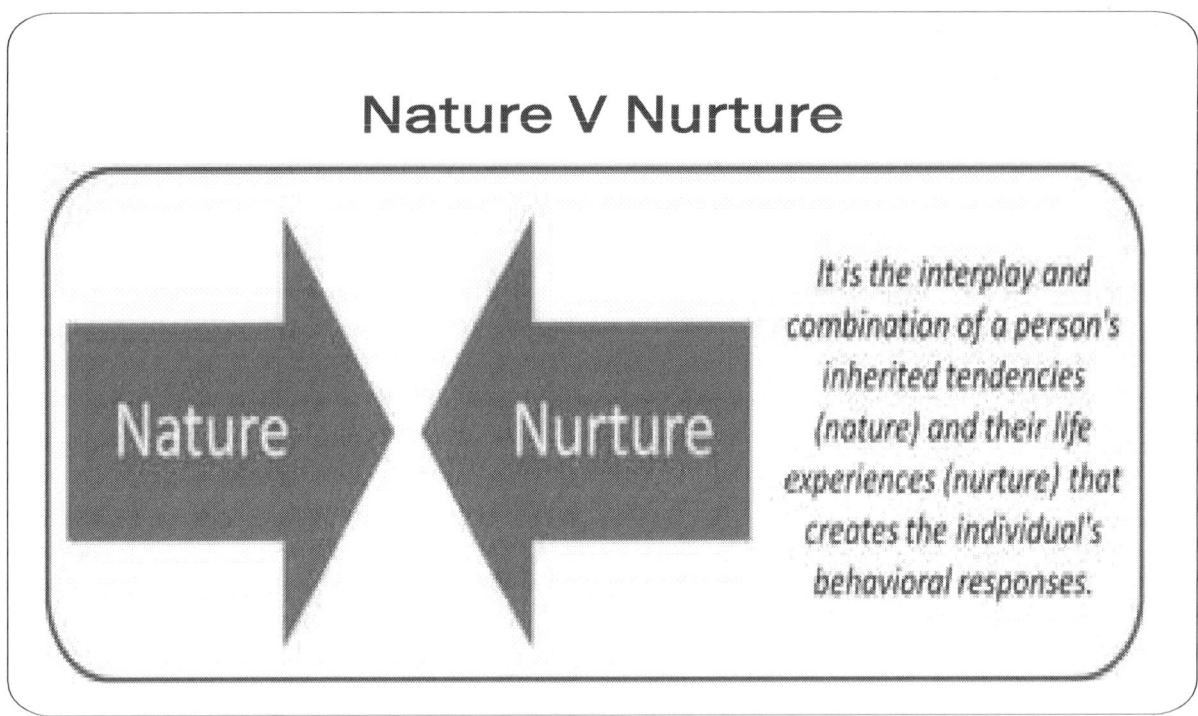

It is the interplay and combination of a person's inherited tendencies (nature) and their life experiences (nurture) that creates the individual's behavioral responses.

It has long been known that certain physical characteristics are biologically determined by genetic inheritance. Colour of eyes, straight or curly hair, pigmentation of the skin and certain diseases (such as Huntingdon's chorea) are all a function of the genes we inherit. Other physical characteristics, if not determined, appear to be at least strongly influenced by the genetic make-up of our biological parents.

Height, weight, hair loss (in men), life expectancy and vulnerability to specific illnesses (e.g. breast cancer in women) are positively correlated between genetically related individuals. These facts have led many to speculate as to whether psychological characteristics such as behavioural tendencies, personality attributes and mental abilities are also "wired in" before we are even born.

Those who adopt an extreme heredity position are known as **nativists**. Their basic assumption is that the characteristics of the human species as a whole are a product of evolution and those individual differences are due to each person's unique genetic code. Characteristics and differences that are not observable at birth, but which emerge later in life, are regarded as the product of maturation. The classic example of the way this affects our physical development are the bodily changes that occur in early adolescence at puberty. Nativists also argue that maturation governs the emergence of attachment in infancy, language acquisition and even cognitive development as a whole.

At the other end of the spectrum are the environmentalists – also known as **empiricists** (not to be confused with the other empirical / scientific approach). Their basic assumption is that at birth the human mind is a **tabula rasa (a blank slate)** and that this is gradually "filled" as a result of experience (e.g. behaviourism). From this point of view psychological characteristics and behavioural differences that emerge through infancy and childhood are the result of learning.

It is how you are brought up (nurture) that governs the psychologically significant aspects of child development and the concept of maturation applies only to the biological. So, when an infant forms an attachment it is responding to the love and attention it has received, language comes from imitating the speech of others and cognitive development depends on the degree of stimulation in the environment and, more broadly, on the civilization within which the child is reared.

Examples of an **extreme nature positions** in psychology include Bowlby's (1969) theory of attachment, which views the bond between mother and child as being an innate process that ensures survival. Likewise, Chomsky (1965) proposed language is gained through the use of an innate language acquisition device. Another example of nature is Freud's theory of aggression as being an innate drive (called thanatos).

In contrast Bandura's (1977) social learning theory states that aggression is learnt from the environment through observation and imitation. This is seen in his famous Bobo doll experiment (Bandura, 1961). Also Skinner (1957) believed that language is learnt from other people via behaviour shaping techniques.

In practice hardly anyone today accepts either of the extreme positions. There are simply too many "facts" on both sides of the argument which are inconsistent with an "all or nothing" view. So instead of asking whether child development is down to nature or nurture the question has been reformulated as **"How much?"**

This question was first framed by Francis Galton (1822-1911) in the late 19th century. Galton (himself a relative of Charles Darwin) was convinced that intellectual ability was largely inherited and that the tendency for "genius" to run in families was the outcome of a natural superiority. This view has cropped up time and again in the history of psychology and has stimulated much of the research into intelligence testing (particularly on separated twins and adopted children). A modern proponent is the American psychologist Arthur Jenson. Finding that the average I.Q. scores of black Americans were significantly lower than whites he went on to argue that genetic factors were mainly responsible – even going so far as to suggest that intelligence is 80% inherited.

The storm of controversy that developed around Jenson's claims was not mainly due to logical and empirical weaknesses in his argument. It was more to do with the **social and political implications that are often drawn from research** that claims to demonstrate natural inequalities between social groups.

Contemporary Views of Nature V's Nurture

Today, the majority of experts believe that behaviour and development are influenced by both nature and nurture. However, the issue still rages on in many areas such as in the debate on the origins of homosexuality and influences on intelligence. While few people take the extreme nativist or empiricist approaches, researchers and experts still debate the degree to which biology and environment influence behaviour.

References:

Baltes, P. B., Reese, H., & Lipsett, L. (1980) Lifespan developmental psychology, *Annual Review of Pyschology 31*: 65 – 110.

Bronfenbrenner, U. (1979). *The Ecology of Human Development: Experiments by Nature and Design*. Cambridge, MA: Harvard University Press. (ISBN 0-674-22457-4)

Buskist, W, C. Heth, C. Schmaltz, R. (2010) Psychology: The Science of Behaviour, Fourth Edition. Oxford University Press

Darwin, C. (1877). A Biographical Sketch of an Infant. *Mind*, 2, 285-294.

Feldman, D, E. Papalia, R, D,(2010). *A child's world : infancy through adolescence* (12th ed. ed.). New York: McGraw-Hill. p. 57. ISBN 9780073532042.

Flaherty, S, C. Sadler,L,S. (2001) "A Review of Attachment Theory in the Context of "Adolescent Parenting". *Journal of Pediatric Health Care* **25** (2): 114 121.:10.1016/j.pedhc.2010.02.005

Freud, S. (1962). *Three Essays on the Theory of Sexuality*, trans. James Strachey. New York: Basic Books.

Kohlberg, L, (1958). "The Development of Modes of Thinking and Choices in Years 10 to 16". *Ph. D. Dissertation, University of Chicago.*

Kohlberg, L (1973). "The Claim to Moral Adequacy of a Highest Stage of Moral Judgment". *Journal of Philosophy* (The Journal of Philosophy, Vol. 70, No. 18) **70** (18): 630–646. 10.2307/2025030.

Lerner, R.M. (2002) *Concepts and theories of human development*. Mahwah, NJ: Erlbaum

McLeod, S, "Erik Erikson". *Simply Psychology*. Retrieved 10 May 2015.

McLeod, S. "Psychosexual Stages". *Simply Psychology*. Retrieved 10 May 2015.

McLeod, S. "Developmental Psychology". *Simply Psychology*. Retrieved 10 May 2015.

Myers, D. (2008). *Exploring Psychology*. Worth Publishers. ISBN 1-57259-096-3.

Neil R, C. Blanchard-Fields, J,C. Cavanaugh, F (2009). *Adult development and aging* (6th ed. ed.). Australia: Wadsworth Cengage Learning. pp. 89–90. ISBN 9780495601746.

Newman, B, M. Newman, P. R. (2011). *Development Through Life : A Psychosocial Approach*. Belmont, CA: Wadsworth Cengage Learning. pp. 215 217.ISBN 111134468X.

Reid, V.; Striano, T. & Koops, W. (2007) *Social Cognition During infancy*. Psychology Press.

Schaie, K. W. (1990). Intellectual development in adulthood. In J. E. Birren & K. W. Schaie (Eds.), Handbook of the psychology of aging, 3rd ed., (pp. 291-309). New York: Academic Press

Siegler, R. (2006). *How Children Develop, Exploring Child Development Student Media Tool Kit & Scientific American Reader to Accompany How Children Develop*. New York: Worth Publishers. ISBN 0-7167-6113-0.

Slater, A.; Lewis, M. (2006). *Introduction to Infant Development*. Oxford: OUP. ISBN 0-19-928305-2.

Smith, P.K.; Cowie, H. & Blades, M. *Understanding Children's Development*. Basic psychology (4 ed.). Oxford, England: Blackwell.

Steinberg, L. (2008). *Adolescence* (8th ed. ed.). Boston: McGraw-Hill Higher Education. pp. 60–365. ISBN 9780073405483.

Upton, P, (2011). *Developmental Psychology: Critical Thinking in Psychology*. Exeter: Learning Matters. p. 62. ISBN 0857252763.

Vygotsky, L.S. (1978). *Mind in Society*. Cambridge, MA: Harvard University Press.

Whiteside, M. Becker, F. (2000). "Parental factors and the young child's post divorce adjustment: A meta-analysis with implications for parenting arrangements." *Journal of Family Psychology* **14** (1): 5–26. :10.1037/0893-3200.14.1.5.

Printed in Great Britain
by Amazon